seize the day

How To Use This Planner

Being a Mum is definitely a juggling act! I designed this planner along with other journals and stationery tools to help me keep my life balanced in all areas of life, whether that's my emotional and spiritual self-love practices, my home & love life and parenting time, my health and fitness or building my home-based business — and of course everyone needs to squeeze in some let-your-hair-down time too!

If you're building a business or starting a project from home whilst the kids are at school you need to make the most of that time — 9 to 3 can fly by. When I started consciously deciding and planning what to do with each of those precious hours, I was amazed at how much more I could get done and how much faster I hit my goals — this is why I decided to share it with other Mum's out there who were also looking to start something new.

Let's start with the Goal Setting section — if you don't think this is a strength at the moment, you're not alone, but it is a skill that you will get better at with practice. If you're not used to setting goals, here are some tips to get you started...

★ Focus on what you want — not what you don't want — and be very specific. You can stretch yourself as long as you believe it's possible.
★ Write your goals in the present tense with a date in the future (the deadline you've given yourself) e.g. "It's the xx of xx, 20xx and I have..."
★ Think about why you want this goal and what will change, for better or worse, if you do or don't achieve it.
★ Visualise yourself accomplishing your goal — how do you feel, what can you see, smell, hear? Make this picture empowering and take a few minutes to focus on it each morning.
★ Look at where you are now and list down what you need to get, do or learn to reach your outcome.
★ Check, review and adjust as you go through your weeks and months.

Right at the beginning of your Planner, there is space dedicated to setting your annual goal(s) as well as room to break it down into bitesize, manageable chunks.

Remember any goals you may have will just be writing on paper without consistent action towards meeting them. That's where your daily habits come into play! Ask yourself what habits will support your goals? And what habits do you currently have which are actively working against you achieving your goals? Releasing habits that no longer serve you are equally as important as setting new ones, for getting you to where you want to be.

At the end of each quarter, these goal and habit pages are repeated to give you the opportunity to reflect and review your progress and adjust them if necessary. Book mark these pages so you can come back to them each day to keep on track.

On to the daily planning section... This should work alongside your diary, not as a diary. It's purpose is for you to assign time to get specific, goal-orientated tasks done.

Before the start of each week, go through your diary and cross out times that are no longer available for you to work on your business e.g., on Tuesday 2 — 4pm, you'll be watching your kids sports match. I suggest you just cross it out rather than write what you're doing as this keeps the page uncluttered and your mind focused on your action steps during your working time... the other stuff belongs in your diary.

Once that's done you can see how much time you have left to dedicate to your business. Decide on your priorities and give each task a fixed, allocated time slot. At the end of each week review the tasks you haven't quite finished and decide whether to ditch, delegate or carry them forward to next week.

 Don't forget your daily wins — these will help motivate you during any low moments and keep your momentum going. Remember even bad days have good moments!

Finally decide on what next week's #1 game-changing goal should be to propel you forward.

Rinse and repeat, keep going — step by step you'll get there and I'm cheering you on all the way!   *Pippa x*

Goal Setting

My #1 Goal for the next 12 months is:

_____

_____

_____

In order to achieve my #1 Goal, I need to:

_____

_____

_____

_____

_____

_____

_____

_____

_____

_____

_____

_____

_____

_____

My #1 Goal for the next 90 days is:

_____

_____

_____

My #1 Goal for month 1:

_____

My #1 Goal for month 2:

_____

My #1 Goal for month 3:

_____

90 Day Habit Tracker

‑‑

‑‑

"*Your emotions are the slaves
to your thoughts,
& you are the slave to your emotions.*"

ELIZABETH GILBERT

‑‑

‑‑

"*A happy mother is a good mother,
& if work makes you hum,
your whole family sings along.*"

SHARON MEERS & JOANNA STROBER

‑‑

‑‑

"*Competent, busy, hurrying people;
it just isn't living at all.*"

ANNE MORROW LINDBERGH

○ ○ ○ ○ ○ ○ ○ ○ ○
○ ○ ○ ○ ○ ○ ○ ○ ○
○ ○ ○ ○ ○ ○ ○ ○ ○
○ ○ ○ ○ ○ ○ ○ ○ ○
○ ○ ○ ○ ○ ○ ○ ○ ○
○ ○ ○ ○ ○ ○ ○ ○ ○
○ ○ ○ ○ ○ ○ ○ ○ ○
○ ○ ○ ○ ○ ○ ○ ○ ○
○ ○ ○ ○ ○ ○ ○ ○ ○

"Be not afraid of growing slowly;
be afraid only of standing still."

CHINESE PROVERB

○ ○ ○ ○ ○ ○ ○ ○ ○
○ ○ ○ ○ ○ ○ ○ ○ ○
○ ○ ○ ○ ○ ○ ○ ○ ○
○ ○ ○ ○ ○ ○ ○ ○ ○
○ ○ ○ ○ ○ ○ ○ ○ ○
○ ○ ○ ○ ○ ○ ○ ○ ○
○ ○ ○ ○ ○ ○ ○ ○ ○
○ ○ ○ ○ ○ ○ ○ ○ ○
○ ○ ○ ○ ○ ○ ○ ○ ○

"Find a group of people who
challenge & inspire you,
spend a lot of time with them,
& it will change your life."

AMY POEHLER

90 Day Habit Release

○ ○ ○ ○ ○ ○ ○ ○ ○
○ ○ ○ ○ ○ ○ ○ ○ ○
○ ○ ○ ○ ○ ○ ○ ○ ○
○ ○ ○ ○ ○ ○ ○ ○ ○
○ ○ ○ ○ ○ ○ ○ ○ ○
○ ○ ○ ○ ○ ○ ○ ○ ○
○ ○ ○ ○ ○ ○ ○ ○ ○
○ ○ ○ ○ ○ ○ ○ ○ ○
○ ○ ○ ○ ○ ○ ○ ○ ○

"First we form habits; then they form us.
Conquer your bad habits,
or they will conquer you."

ROB GILBERT

MONDAY	
TIME:	**ACTION:**
am	
9am	
10am	
11am	
12pm	
1pm	
2pm	

Evening:

Dinner:

todays win

TUESDAY	
TIME:	**ACTION:**
am	
9am	
10am	
11am	
12pm	
1pm	
2pm	

Evening:

Dinner:

todays win

WEDNESDAY		THURSDAY	
TIME:	**ACTION:**	**TIME:**	**ACTION:**
am		am	Rose + Reuben School
9am		9am	
10am		10am	
11am		11am	
12pm		12pm	
1pm		1pm	
2pm		2pm	

Evening:

Evening:

Dinner:

Dinner:

todays win

todays win

FRIDAY

TIME:	ACTION:
am	
9am	
10am	
11am	
12pm	
1pm	
2pm	

Evening:

Dinner:

todays win

WEEKEND:

TIME:	ACTION:

DITCH, DELEGATE, DO NEXT WEEK:

Next weeks #1 Goal

weekend wins

MONDAY		TUESDAY	
TIME:	**ACTION:**	**TIME:**	**ACTION:**
am		am	
9am		9am	
10am		10am	
11am		11am	
12pm		12pm	
1pm		1pm	
2pm		2pm	

Evening:

Evening:

Dinner:

Dinner:

todays win

todays win

WEDNESDAY		THURSDAY	
TIME:	**ACTION:**	**TIME:**	**ACTION:**
am		am	
9am		9am	
10am		10am	
11am		11am	
12pm		12pm	
1pm		1pm	
2pm		2pm	

Evening:

Evening:

Dinner:

Dinner:

todays win

todays win

FRIDAY

TIME:	ACTION:
am	
9am	
10am	
11am	
12pm	
1pm	
2pm	

Evening:

Dinner:

todays win

WEEKEND:

TIME:	ACTION:

DITCH, DELEGATE, DO NEXT WEEK:

Next weeks #1 Goal

weekend wins

MONDAY

TIME:	ACTION:
am	
9am	
10am	
11am	
12pm	
1pm	
2pm	

Evening:

Dinner:

todays win

TUESDAY

TIME:	ACTION:
am	
9am	
10am	
11am	
12pm	
1pm	
2pm	

Evening:

Dinner:

todays win

WEDNESDAY		THURSDAY	
TIME:	**ACTION:**	**TIME:**	**ACTION:**
am		am	
9am		9am	
10am		10am	
11am		11am	
12pm		12pm	
1pm		1pm	
2pm		2pm	

Evening:

Evening:

Dinner:

Dinner:

todays win

todays win

FRIDAY

TIME:	ACTION:
am	
9am	
10am	
11am	
12pm	
1pm	
2pm	

Evening:

Dinner:

todays win

WEEKEND:

TIME:	ACTION:

DITCH, DELEGATE, DO NEXT WEEK:

Next weeks #1 Goal

weekend wins

MONDAY		TUESDAY	
TIME:	**ACTION:**	**TIME:**	**ACTION:**
am		am	
9am		9am	
10am		10am	
11am		11am	
12pm		12pm	
1pm		1pm	
2pm		2pm	

Evening:

Dinner:

Evening:

Dinner:

todays win

todays win

WEDNESDAY

TIME:	ACTION:
am	
9am	
10am	
11am	
12pm	
1pm	
2pm	

Evening:

Dinner:

todays win

THURSDAY

TIME:	ACTION:
am	
9am	
10am	
11am	
12pm	
1pm	
2pm	

Evening:

Dinner:

todays win

FRIDAY		WEEKEND:	
TIME:	**ACTION:**	**TIME:**	**ACTION:**
am			
9am			
10am			
11am			

DITCH, DELEGATE, DO NEXT WEEK:

12pm			
1pm			
2pm			

Evening:

Next weeks
#1
Goal

Dinner:

todays win

weekend wins

MONDAY

TIME:	ACTION:
am	
9am	
10am	
11am	
12pm	
1pm	
2pm	

Evening:

Dinner:

todays win

TUESDAY

TIME:	ACTION:
am	
9am	
10am	
11am	
12pm	
1pm	
2pm	

Evening:

Dinner:

todays win

WEDNESDAY		THURSDAY	
TIME:	**ACTION:**	**TIME:**	**ACTION:**
am		am	
9am		9am	
10am		10am	
11am		11am	
12pm		12pm	
1pm		1pm	
2pm		2pm	

Evening:

Evening:

Dinner:

Dinner:

todays *win*   *todays* *win*

FRIDAY

TIME:	ACTION:
am	
9am	
10am	
11am	
12pm	
1pm	
2pm	

Evening:

Dinner:

todays win

WEEKEND:

TIME:	ACTION:

DITCH, DELEGATE, DO NEXT WEEK:

Next weeks #1 Goal

weekend wins

MONDAY		TUESDAY	
TIME:	**ACTION:**	**TIME:**	**ACTION:**
am		am	
9am		9am	
10am		10am	
11am		11am	
12pm		12pm	
1pm		1pm	
2pm		2pm	

Evening: **Evening:**

Dinner: **Dinner:**

todays win   *todays win*

WEDNESDAY	
TIME:	**ACTION:**
am	
9am	
10am	
11am	
12pm	
1pm	
2pm	

Evening:

Dinner:

todays win

THURSDAY	
TIME:	**ACTION:**
am	
9am	
10am	
11am	
12pm	
1pm	
2pm	

Evening:

Dinner:

todays win

FRIDAY		WEEKEND:	
TIME:	**ACTION:**	**TIME:**	**ACTION:**
am			
9am			
10am			
11am			

DITCH, DELEGATE, DO NEXT WEEK:

12pm			
1pm			
2pm			

Evening:

Dinner:

Next weeks #1 Goal

todays win

weekend wins

MONDAY		TUESDAY	
TIME:	**ACTION:**	**TIME:**	**ACTION:**
am		am	
9am		9am	
10am		10am	
11am		11am	
12pm		12pm	
1pm		1pm	
2pm		2pm	

Evening:

Evening:

Dinner:

Dinner:

todays win

todays win

WEDNESDAY		THURSDAY	
TIME:	ACTION:	TIME:	ACTION:
am		am	
9am		9am	
10am		10am	
11am		11am	
12pm		12pm	
1pm		1pm	
2pm		2pm	

Evening:

Evening:

Dinner:

Dinner:

todays win

todays win

FRIDAY		WEEKEND:	
TIME:	ACTION:	TIME:	ACTION:
am			
9am			
10am			
11am			

DITCH, DELEGATE, DO NEXT WEEK:

FRIDAY	
12pm	
1pm	
2pm	

Evening:

Dinner:

todays win

Next weeks #1 Goal

weekend wins

MONDAY		TUESDAY	
TIME:	**ACTION:**	**TIME:**	**ACTION:**
am		am	
9am		9am	
10am		10am	
11am		11am	
12pm		12pm	
1pm		1pm	
2pm		2pm	

Evening:

Evening:

Dinner:

Dinner:

todays win

todays win

WEDNESDAY		THURSDAY	
TIME:	**ACTION:**	**TIME:**	**ACTION:**
am		am	
9am		9am	
10am		10am	
11am		11am	
12pm		12pm	
1pm		1pm	
2pm		2pm	

Evening:

Dinner:

Evening:

Dinner:

todays win

todays win

FRIDAY		WEEKEND:	
TIME:	**ACTION:**	**TIME:**	**ACTION:**
am			
9am			
10am			
11am			

DITCH, DELEGATE, DO NEXT WEEK:

FRIDAY	
12pm	
1pm	
2pm	

Evening:

Next weeks #1 Goal

Dinner:

todays win

weekend wins

MONDAY		TUESDAY	
TIME:	**ACTION:**	**TIME:**	**ACTION:**
am		**am**	
9am		**9am**	
10am		**10am**	
11am		**11am**	
12pm		**12pm**	
1pm		**1pm**	
2pm		**2pm**	

Evening:

Dinner:

Evening:

Dinner:

todays win

todays win

WEDNESDAY	
TIME:	ACTION:
am	
9am	
10am	
11am	
12pm	
1pm	
2pm	

Evening:

Dinner:

todays win

THURSDAY	
TIME:	ACTION:
am	
9am	
10am	
11am	
12pm	
1pm	
2pm	

Evening:

Dinner:

todays win

FRIDAY		WEEKEND:	
TIME:	**ACTION:**	**TIME:**	**ACTION:**
am			
9am			
10am			
11am			

DITCH, DELEGATE, DO NEXT WEEK:

FRIDAY	
12pm	
1pm	
2pm	

Evening:

Dinner:

Next weeks #1 Goal

todays win

weekend wins

MONDAY			TUESDAY	
TIME:	**ACTION:**		**TIME:**	**ACTION:**
am			am	
9am			9am	
10am			10am	
11am			11am	
12pm			12pm	
1pm			1pm	
2pm			2pm	

Evening:

Dinner:

todays win

Evening:

Dinner:

todays win

WEDNESDAY	
TIME:	**ACTION:**
am	
9am	
10am	
11am	
12pm	
1pm	
2pm	

Evening:

Dinner:

todays win

THURSDAY	
TIME:	**ACTION:**
am	
9am	
10am	
11am	
12pm	
1pm	
2pm	

Evening:

Dinner:

todays win

FRIDAY		WEEKEND:	
TIME:	ACTION:	TIME:	ACTION:
am			
9am			
10am			
11am			

DITCH, DELEGATE, DO NEXT WEEK:

12pm		
1pm		
2pm		

Evening:

Next weeks #1 Goal

Dinner:

todays win

weekend wins

MONDAY

TIME:	ACTION:
am	
9am	
10am	
11am	
12pm	
1pm	
2pm	

Evening:

Dinner:

todays win

TUESDAY

TIME:	ACTION:
am	
9am	
10am	
11am	
12pm	
1pm	
2pm	

Evening:

Dinner:

todays win

WEDNESDAY

TIME:	ACTION:
am	
9am	
10am	
11am	
12pm	
1pm	
2pm	

Evening:

Dinner:

todays win

THURSDAY

TIME:	ACTION:
am	
9am	
10am	
11am	
12pm	
1pm	
2pm	

Evening:

Dinner:

todays win

FRIDAY

TIME:	ACTION:
am	
9am	
10am	
11am	
12pm	
1pm	
2pm	

Evening:

Dinner:

todays win

WEEKEND:

TIME:	ACTION:

DITCH, DELEGATE, DO NEXT WEEK:

Next weeks #1 Goal

weekend wins

MONDAY		TUESDAY	
TIME:	**ACTION:**	**TIME:**	**ACTION:**
am		am	
9am		9am	
10am		10am	
11am		11am	
12pm		12pm	
1pm		1pm	
2pm		2pm	

Evening:

Evening:

Dinner:

Dinner:

todays win

todays win

WEDNESDAY		THURSDAY	
TIME:	ACTION:	TIME:	ACTION:
am		am	
9am		9am	
10am		10am	
11am		11am	
12pm		12pm	
1pm		1pm	
2pm		2pm	

Evening:

Dinner:

todays win

Evening:

Dinner:

todays win

FRIDAY		WEEKEND:	
TIME:	**ACTION:**	**TIME:**	**ACTION:**
am			
9am			
10am			
11am			
		DITCH, DELEGATE, DO NEXT WEEK:	
12pm			
1pm			
2pm			

Evening:

Dinner:

todays win

Next weeks #1 goal

weekend wins

MONDAY

TIME:	ACTION:
am	
9am	
10am	
11am	
12pm	
1pm	
2pm	

Evening:

Dinner:

todays win

TUESDAY

TIME:	ACTION:
am	
9am	
10am	
11am	
12pm	
1pm	
2pm	

Evening:

Dinner:

todays win

WEDNESDAY		THURSDAY	
TIME:	**ACTION:**	**TIME:**	**ACTION:**
am		am	
9am		9am	
10am		10am	
11am		11am	
12pm		12pm	
1pm		1pm	
2pm		2pm	

Evening:

Evening:

Dinner:

Dinner:

todays win

todays win

FRIDAY		WEEKEND:	
TIME:	ACTION:	TIME:	ACTION:
am			
9am			
10am			
11am			
		DITCH, DELEGATE, DO NEXT WEEK:	
12pm			
1pm			
2pm			

Evening:

Dinner:

Next weeks #1 Goal

todays win

weekend wins

MONDAY		TUESDAY	
TIME:	**ACTION:**	**TIME:**	**ACTION:**
am		am	
9am		9am	
10am		10am	
11am		11am	
12pm		12pm	
1pm		1pm	
2pm		2pm	

Evening:

Evening:

Dinner:

Dinner:

todays win

todays win

WEDNESDAY		THURSDAY	
TIME:	**ACTION:**	**TIME:**	**ACTION:**
am		am	
9am		9am	
10am		10am	
11am		11am	
12pm		12pm	
1pm		1pm	
2pm		2pm	

Evening:

Dinner:

Evening:

Dinner:

todays win

todays win

FRIDAY		WEEKEND:	
TIME:	**ACTION:**	**TIME:**	**ACTION:**
am			
9am			
10am			
11am			

DITCH, DELEGATE, DO NEXT WEEK:

12pm			
1pm			
2pm			

Evening:

Next weeks #1 Goal

Dinner:

todays win

weekend wins

MONDAY

TIME:	ACTION:
am	
9am	
10am	
11am	
12pm	
1pm	
2pm	

Evening:

Dinner:

todays win

TUESDAY

TIME:	ACTION:
am	
9am	
10am	
11am	
12pm	
1pm	
2pm	

Evening:

Dinner:

todays win

WEDNESDAY	**THURSDAY**

TIME:	ACTION:	TIME:	ACTION:
am		am	
9am		9am	
10am		10am	
11am		11am	
12pm		12pm	
1pm		1pm	
2pm		2pm	

Evening:

Evening:

Dinner:

Dinner:

todays win

todays win

FRIDAY		WEEKEND:	
TIME:	**ACTION:**	**TIME:**	**ACTION:**
am			
9am			
10am			
11am			
		DITCH, DELEGATE, DO NEXT WEEK:	
12pm			
1pm			
2pm			

Evening:

Dinner:

Next weeks #1 Goal

todays win

weekend wins

Goal Setting, Reflection & Review

What was my #1 Goal for this 12 months?

_____

_____

Have I achieved the goals I set for months 1, 2 & 3?

_____

_____

My key wins have been:

_____

_____

My key challenges have been:

_____

_____

My key learnings are:

_____

_____

Do I need to adjust my 12 month #1 Goal?

_____

_____

My #1 Goal for the next 90 days is:

_____

_____

My #1 Goal for month 4:

_____

My #1 Goal for month 5:

_____

My #1 Goal for month 6:

_____

90 Day Habit Tracker

○ ○ ○ ○ ○ ○ ○ ○ ○ ○
○ ○ ○ ○ ○ ○ ○ ○ ○ ○
○ ○ ○ ○ ○ ○ ○ ○ ○ ○
○ ○ ○ ○ ○ ○ ○ ○ ○ ○
○ ○ ○ ○ ○ ○ ○ ○ ○ ○
○ ○ ○ ○ ○ ○ ○ ○ ○ ○
○ ○ ○ ○ ○ ○ ○ ○ ○ ○
○ ○ ○ ○ ○ ○ ○ ○ ○ ○
○ ○ ○ ○ ○ ○ ○ ○ ○ ○

*"You have been assigned this mountain
to show others it can be moved."*

ANONYMOUS

○ ○ ○ ○ ○ ○ ○ ○ ○ ○
○ ○ ○ ○ ○ ○ ○ ○ ○ ○
○ ○ ○ ○ ○ ○ ○ ○ ○ ○
○ ○ ○ ○ ○ ○ ○ ○ ○ ○
○ ○ ○ ○ ○ ○ ○ ○ ○ ○
○ ○ ○ ○ ○ ○ ○ ○ ○ ○
○ ○ ○ ○ ○ ○ ○ ○ ○ ○
○ ○ ○ ○ ○ ○ ○ ○ ○ ○
○ ○ ○ ○ ○ ○ ○ ○ ○ ○

*" You can't do anything about
the length of your life,
but you can do something about
its width & it's depth."*

SHIRA TEHRANI

○ ○ ○ ○ ○ ○ ○ ○ ○ ○
○ ○ ○ ○ ○ ○ ○ ○ ○ ○
○ ○ ○ ○ ○ ○ ○ ○ ○ ○
○ ○ ○ ○ ○ ○ ○ ○ ○ ○
○ ○ ○ ○ ○ ○ ○ ○ ○ ○
○ ○ ○ ○ ○ ○ ○ ○ ○ ○
○ ○ ○ ○ ○ ○ ○ ○ ○ ○
○ ○ ○ ○ ○ ○ ○ ○ ○ ○
○ ○ ○ ○ ○ ○ ○ ○ ○ ○

*"In order to be in control of your life, you
have to have a purpose –
a productive purpose."*

AYN RAND

○ ○ ○ ○ ○ ○ ○ ○ ○ ○
○ ○ ○ ○ ○ ○ ○ ○ ○ ○
○ ○ ○ ○ ○ ○ ○ ○ ○ ○
○ ○ ○ ○ ○ ○ ○ ○ ○ ○
○ ○ ○ ○ ○ ○ ○ ○ ○ ○
○ ○ ○ ○ ○ ○ ○ ○ ○ ○
○ ○ ○ ○ ○ ○ ○ ○ ○ ○
○ ○ ○ ○ ○ ○ ○ ○ ○ ○
○ ○ ○ ○ ○ ○ ○ ○ ○ ○

*"Knowing what you want
is the first step in getting it."*

LOUISE HART

○ ○ ○ ○ ○ ○ ○ ○ ○ ○
○ ○ ○ ○ ○ ○ ○ ○ ○ ○
○ ○ ○ ○ ○ ○ ○ ○ ○ ○
○ ○ ○ ○ ○ ○ ○ ○ ○ ○
○ ○ ○ ○ ○ ○ ○ ○ ○ ○
○ ○ ○ ○ ○ ○ ○ ○ ○ ○
○ ○ ○ ○ ○ ○ ○ ○ ○ ○
○ ○ ○ ○ ○ ○ ○ ○ ○ ○
○ ○ ○ ○ ○ ○ ○ ○ ○ ○

*"Love is a two-way street,
constantly under construction."*

CARROLL BRYANT

90 Day Habit Release

○ ○ ○ ○ ○ ○ ○ ○ ○ ○
○ ○ ○ ○ ○ ○ ○ ○ ○ ○
○ ○ ○ ○ ○ ○ ○ ○ ○ ○
○ ○ ○ ○ ○ ○ ○ ○ ○ ○
○ ○ ○ ○ ○ ○ ○ ○ ○ ○
○ ○ ○ ○ ○ ○ ○ ○ ○ ○
○ ○ ○ ○ ○ ○ ○ ○ ○ ○
○ ○ ○ ○ ○ ○ ○ ○ ○ ○
○ ○ ○ ○ ○ ○ ○ ○ ○ ○

*"If habits don't line up with your dream,
then you either need to change your habits or
change your dream."*

JOHN MAXWELL

MONDAY			TUESDAY	
TIME:	**ACTION:**		**TIME:**	**ACTION:**
am			am	
9am			9am	
10am			10am	
11am			11am	
12pm			12pm	
1pm			1pm	
2pm			2pm	

Evening:

Dinner:

Evening:

Dinner:

todays win

todays win

WEDNESDAY

TIME:	ACTION:
am	
9am	
10am	
11am	
12pm	
1pm	
2pm	

Evening:

Dinner:

todays win

THURSDAY

TIME:	ACTION:
am	
9am	
10am	
11am	
12pm	
1pm	
2pm	

Evening:

Dinner:

todays win

FRIDAY

TIME:	ACTION:
am	
9am	
10am	
11am	
12pm	
1pm	
2pm	

Evening:

Dinner:

todays win

WEEKEND:

TIME:	ACTION:

DITCH, DELEGATE, DO NEXT WEEK:

Next weeks #1 Goal

weekend wins

MONDAY		TUESDAY	
TIME:	**ACTION:**	**TIME:**	**ACTION:**
am		am	
9am		9am	
10am		10am	
11am		11am	
12pm		12pm	
1pm		1pm	
2pm		2pm	

Evening:

Dinner:

Evening:

Dinner:

todays win

todays win

WEDNESDAY		THURSDAY	
TIME:	ACTION:	TIME:	ACTION:
am		am	
9am		9am	
10am		10am	
11am		11am	
12pm		12pm	
1pm		1pm	
2pm		2pm	

Evening:

Evening:

Dinner:

Dinner:

todays win

todays win

FRIDAY		WEEKEND:	
TIME:	**ACTION:**	**TIME:**	**ACTION:**
am			
9am			
10am			
11am			
		DITCH, DELEGATE, DO NEXT WEEK:	
12pm			
1pm			
2pm			

Evening:

Dinner:

todays win

Next weeks #1 Goal

weekend wins

MONDAY		TUESDAY	
TIME:	**ACTION:**	**TIME:**	**ACTION:**
am		am	
9am		9am	
10am		10am	
11am		11am	
12pm		12pm	
1pm		1pm	
2pm		2pm	

Evening:

Evening:

Dinner:

Dinner:

todays win

todays win

WEDNESDAY

TIME:	ACTION:
am	
9am	
10am	
11am	
12pm	
1pm	
2pm	

Evening:

Dinner:

todays win

THURSDAY

TIME:	ACTION:
am	
9am	
10am	
11am	
12pm	
1pm	
2pm	

Evening:

Dinner:

todays win

FRIDAY		WEEKEND:	
TIME:	**ACTION:**	**TIME:**	**ACTION:**
am			
9am			
10am			
11am			

DITCH, DELEGATE, DO NEXT WEEK:

12pm			
1pm			
2pm			

Evening:

Next weeks
#1
goal

Dinner:

todays
win

weekend
wins

MONDAY		TUESDAY	
TIME:	**ACTION:**	**TIME:**	**ACTION:**
am		am	
9am		9am	
10am		10am	
11am		11am	
12pm		12pm	
1pm		1pm	
2pm		2pm	

Evening:

Evening:

Dinner:

Dinner:

todays win

todays win

WEDNESDAY		THURSDAY	
TIME:	**ACTION:**	**TIME:**	**ACTION:**
am		am	
9am		9am	
10am		10am	
11am		11am	
12pm		12pm	
1pm		1pm	
2pm		2pm	

Evening:

Evening:

Dinner:

Dinner:

todays win

todays win

FRIDAY

TIME:	ACTION:
am	
9am	
10am	
11am	
12pm	
1pm	
2pm	

Evening:

Dinner:

todays win

WEEKEND:

TIME:	ACTION:

DITCH, DELEGATE, DO NEXT WEEK:

Next weeks #1 Goal

weekend wins

MONDAY		TUESDAY	
TIME:	**ACTION:**	**TIME:**	**ACTION:**
am		am	
9am		9am	
10am		10am	
11am		11am	
12pm		12pm	
1pm		1pm	
2pm		2pm	

Evening:

Evening:

Dinner:

Dinner:

todays win

todays win

WEDNESDAY		THURSDAY	
TIME:	**ACTION:**	**TIME:**	**ACTION:**
am		am	
9am		9am	
10am		10am	
11am		11am	
12pm		12pm	
1pm		1pm	
2pm		2pm	

Evening:

Evening:

Dinner:

Dinner:

todays win

todays win

FRIDAY		WEEKEND:	
TIME:	**ACTION:**	**TIME:**	**ACTION:**
am			
9am			
10am			
11am			

DITCH, DELEGATE, DO NEXT WEEK:

FRIDAY		
12pm		
1pm		
2pm		

Evening:

Next weeks
#1
Goal

Dinner:

todays win

weekend wins

MONDAY		TUESDAY	
TIME:	**ACTION:**	**TIME:**	**ACTION:**
am		am	
9am		9am	
10am		10am	
11am		11am	
12pm		12pm	
1pm		1pm	
2pm		2pm	

Evening:

Dinner:

Evening:

Dinner:

todays win

todays win

WEDNESDAY

TIME:	ACTION:
am	
9am	
10am	
11am	
12pm	
1pm	
2pm	

Evening:

Dinner:

todays win

THURSDAY

TIME:	ACTION:
am	
9am	
10am	
11am	
12pm	
1pm	
2pm	

Evening:

Dinner:

todays win

FRIDAY

TIME:	ACTION:
am	
9am	
10am	
11am	
12pm	
1pm	
2pm	

Evening:

Dinner:

todays win

WEEKEND:

TIME:	ACTION:

DITCH, DELEGATE, DO NEXT WEEK:

Next weeks #1 Goal

weekend wins

MONDAY		TUESDAY	
TIME:	**ACTION:**	**TIME:**	**ACTION:**
am		am	
9am		9am	
10am		10am	
11am		11am	
12pm		12pm	
1pm		1pm	
2pm		2pm	

Evening:

Evening:

Dinner:

Dinner:

todays win

todays win

WEDNESDAY		THURSDAY	
TIME:	**ACTION:**	**TIME:**	**ACTION:**
am		am	
9am		9am	
10am		10am	
11am		11am	
12pm		12pm	
1pm		1pm	
2pm		2pm	

Evening:

Dinner:

Evening:

Dinner:

todays win

todays win

FRIDAY

TIME:	ACTION:
am	
9am	
10am	
11am	
12pm	
1pm	
2pm	

Evening:

Dinner:

todays win

WEEKEND:

TIME:	ACTION:

DITCH, DELEGATE, DO NEXT WEEK:

Next weeks #1 Goal

weekend wins

MONDAY		TUESDAY	
TIME:	**ACTION:**	**TIME:**	**ACTION:**
am		am	
9am		9am	
10am		10am	
11am		11am	
12pm		12pm	
1pm		1pm	
2pm		2pm	

Evening:

Evening:

Dinner:

Dinner:

todays win

todays win

WEDNESDAY		THURSDAY	
TIME:	**ACTION:**	**TIME:**	**ACTION:**
am		am	
9am		9am	
10am		10am	
11am		11am	
12pm		12pm	
1pm		1pm	
2pm		2pm	

Evening:

Evening:

Dinner:

Dinner:

todays win

todays win

FRIDAY

TIME:	ACTION:
am	
9am	
10am	
11am	
12pm	
1pm	
2pm	

Evening:

Dinner:

todays win

WEEKEND:

TIME:	ACTION:

DITCH, DELEGATE, DO NEXT WEEK:

Next weeks #1 Goal

weekend wins

MONDAY		TUESDAY	
TIME:	**ACTION:**	**TIME:**	**ACTION:**
am		am	
9am		9am	
10am		10am	
11am		11am	
12pm		12pm	
1pm		1pm	
2pm		2pm	

Evening:

Evening:

Dinner:

Dinner:

todays win

todays win

WEDNESDAY

TIME:	ACTION:
am	
9am	
10am	
11am	
12pm	
1pm	
2pm	

Evening:

Dinner:

todays win

THURSDAY

TIME:	ACTION:
am	
9am	
10am	
11am	
12pm	
1pm	
2pm	

Evening:

Dinner:

todays win

FRIDAY		WEEKEND:	
TIME:	**ACTION:**	**TIME:**	**ACTION:**
am			
9am			
10am			
11am			

DITCH, DELEGATE, DO NEXT WEEK:

FRIDAY	
12pm	
1pm	
2pm	

Evening:

Dinner:

Next weeks #1 Goal

todays win

weekend wins

MONDAY		TUESDAY	
TIME:	**ACTION:**	**TIME:**	**ACTION:**
am		am	
9am		9am	
10am		10am	
11am		11am	
12pm		12pm	
1pm		1pm	
2pm		2pm	

Evening:

Dinner:

Evening:

Dinner:

todays win

todays win

WEDNESDAY		THURSDAY	
TIME:	**ACTION:**	**TIME:**	**ACTION:**
am		am	
9am		9am	
10am		10am	
11am		11am	
12pm		12pm	
1pm		1pm	
2pm		2pm	

Evening:

Dinner:

todays win

Evening:

Dinner:

todays win

FRIDAY		WEEKEND:	
TIME:	**ACTION:**	**TIME:**	**ACTION:**
am			
9am			
10am			
11am			
		DITCH, DELEGATE, DO NEXT WEEK:	
12pm			
1pm			
2pm			

Evening:

Dinner:

Next weeks #1 Goal

todays win

weekend wins

MONDAY		TUESDAY	
TIME:	**ACTION:**	**TIME:**	**ACTION:**
am		am	
9am		9am	
10am		10am	
11am		11am	
12pm		12pm	
1pm		1pm	
2pm		2pm	

Evening:

Evening:

Dinner:

Dinner:

todays win

todays win

WEDNESDAY		THURSDAY	
TIME:	**ACTION:**	**TIME:**	**ACTION:**
am		am	
9am		9am	
10am		10am	
11am		11am	
12pm		12pm	
1pm		1pm	
2pm		2pm	

Evening:

Evening:

Dinner:

Dinner:

todays win

todays win

FRIDAY		WEEKEND:	
TIME:	**ACTION:**	**TIME:**	**ACTION:**
am			
9am			
10am			
11am			

DITCH, DELEGATE, DO NEXT WEEK:

12pm	
1pm	
2pm	

Evening:

Dinner:

todays win

Next weeks #1 Goal

weekend wins

MONDAY		TUESDAY	
TIME:	**ACTION:**	**TIME:**	**ACTION:**
am		am	
9am		9am	
10am		10am	
11am		11am	
12pm		12pm	
1pm		1pm	
2pm		2pm	

Evening:

Evening:

Dinner:

Dinner:

todays win

todays win

WEDNESDAY		THURSDAY	
TIME:	**ACTION:**	**TIME:**	**ACTION:**
am		am	
9am		9am	
10am		10am	
11am		11am	
12pm		12pm	
1pm		1pm	
2pm		2pm	

Evening:

Evening:

Dinner:

Dinner:

todays win

todays win

FRIDAY

TIME:	ACTION:
am	
9am	
10am	
11am	
12pm	
1pm	
2pm	

Evening:

Dinner:

todays win

WEEKEND:

TIME:	ACTION:

DITCH, DELEGATE, DO NEXT WEEK:

Next weeks #1 Goal

weekend wins

MONDAY

TIME:	ACTION:
am	
9am	
10am	
11am	
12pm	
1pm	
2pm	

Evening:

Dinner:

todays win

TUESDAY

TIME:	ACTION:
am	
9am	
10am	
11am	
12pm	
1pm	
2pm	

Evening:

Dinner:

todays win

WEDNESDAY		THURSDAY	
TIME:	**ACTION:**	**TIME:**	**ACTION:**
am		am	
9am		9am	
10am		10am	
11am		11am	
12pm		12pm	
1pm		1pm	
2pm		2pm	

Evening:

Evening:

Dinner:

Dinner:

todays win

todays win

FRIDAY		WEEKEND:	
TIME:	**ACTION:**	**TIME:**	**ACTION:**
am			
9am			
10am			
11am			

DITCH, DELEGATE, DO NEXT WEEK:

12pm			
1pm			
2pm			

Evening:

Next weeks #1 Goal

Dinner:

todays win

weekend wins

MONDAY		TUESDAY	
TIME:	**ACTION:**	**TIME:**	**ACTION:**
am		am	
9am		9am	
10am		10am	
11am		11am	
12pm		12pm	
1pm		1pm	
2pm		2pm	

Evening:

Evening:

Dinner:

Dinner:

todays win

todays win

WEDNESDAY

TIME:	ACTION:
am	
9am	
10am	
11am	
12pm	
1pm	
2pm	

Evening:

Dinner:

todays win

THURSDAY

TIME:	ACTION:
am	
9am	
10am	
11am	
12pm	
1pm	
2pm	

Evening:

Dinner:

todays win

FRIDAY		WEEKEND:	
TIME:	**ACTION:**	**TIME:**	**ACTION:**
am			
9am			
10am			
11am			
		DITCH, DELEGATE, DO NEXT WEEK:	
12pm			
1pm			
2pm			

Evening:

Dinner:

todays win

Next weeks #1 Goal

weekend wins

MONDAY		TUESDAY	
TIME:	**ACTION:**	**TIME:**	**ACTION:**
am		am	
9am		9am	
10am		10am	
11am		11am	
12pm		12pm	
1pm		1pm	
2pm		2pm	

Evening:

Evening:

Dinner:

Dinner:

todays win

todays win

WEDNESDAY		THURSDAY	
TIME:	**ACTION:**	**TIME:**	**ACTION:**
am		am	
9am		9am	
10am		10am	
11am		11am	
12pm		12pm	
1pm		1pm	
2pm		2pm	

Evening:

Evening:

Dinner:

Dinner:

todays win

todays win

FRIDAY		WEEKEND:	
TIME:	**ACTION:**	**TIME:**	**ACTION:**
am			
9am			
10am			
11am			

	DITCH, DELEGATE, DO NEXT WEEK:
12pm	
1pm	
2pm	

Evening:

Next weeks #1 Goal

Dinner:

todays win

weekend wins

Goal Setting, Reflection & Review

What was my #1 Goal for this 12 months?

_____

_____

Have I achieved the goals I set for months 4, 5 & 6?

_____

_____

My key wins have been:

_____

_____

My key challenges have been:

_____

_____

My key learnings are:

_____

_____

_____

Do I need to adjust my 12 month #1 Goal?

_____

_____

My #1 Goal for the next 90 days is:

_____

_____

My #1 Goal for month 7:

_____

My #1 Goal for month 8:

_____

My #1 Goal for month 9:

_____

90 Day Habit Tracker

○ ○ ○ ○ ○ ○ ○ ○ ○ ○
○ ○ ○ ○ ○ ○ ○ ○ ○ ○
○ ○ ○ ○ ○ ○ ○ ○ ○ ○
○ ○ ○ ○ ○ ○ ○ ○ ○ ○
○ ○ ○ ○ ○ ○ ○ ○ ○ ○
○ ○ ○ ○ ○ ○ ○ ○ ○ ○
○ ○ ○ ○ ○ ○ ○ ○ ○ ○
○ ○ ○ ○ ○ ○ ○ ○ ○ ○
○ ○ ○ ○ ○ ○ ○ ○ ○ ○

*"Some pursue happiness,
others create it."*

ANONYMOUS

○ ○ ○ ○ ○ ○ ○ ○ ○ ○
○ ○ ○ ○ ○ ○ ○ ○ ○ ○
○ ○ ○ ○ ○ ○ ○ ○ ○ ○
○ ○ ○ ○ ○ ○ ○ ○ ○ ○
○ ○ ○ ○ ○ ○ ○ ○ ○ ○
○ ○ ○ ○ ○ ○ ○ ○ ○ ○
○ ○ ○ ○ ○ ○ ○ ○ ○ ○
○ ○ ○ ○ ○ ○ ○ ○ ○ ○
○ ○ ○ ○ ○ ○ ○ ○ ○ ○

*"There are many ways to measure success;
not the least of which is
the way your child describes you,
when talking to a friend."*

ANONYMOUS

○ ○ ○ ○ ○ ○ ○ ○ ○ ○
○ ○ ○ ○ ○ ○ ○ ○ ○ ○
○ ○ ○ ○ ○ ○ ○ ○ ○ ○
○ ○ ○ ○ ○ ○ ○ ○ ○ ○
○ ○ ○ ○ ○ ○ ○ ○ ○ ○
○ ○ ○ ○ ○ ○ ○ ○ ○ ○
○ ○ ○ ○ ○ ○ ○ ○ ○ ○
○ ○ ○ ○ ○ ○ ○ ○ ○ ○
○ ○ ○ ○ ○ ○ ○ ○ ○ ○

*"Life is either a daring adventure
or nothing."*

HELEN KELLER

○ ○ ○ ○ ○ ○ ○ ○ ○ ○
○ ○ ○ ○ ○ ○ ○ ○ ○ ○
○ ○ ○ ○ ○ ○ ○ ○ ○ ○
○ ○ ○ ○ ○ ○ ○ ○ ○ ○
○ ○ ○ ○ ○ ○ ○ ○ ○ ○
○ ○ ○ ○ ○ ○ ○ ○ ○ ○
○ ○ ○ ○ ○ ○ ○ ○ ○ ○
○ ○ ○ ○ ○ ○ ○ ○ ○ ○
○ ○ ○ ○ ○ ○ ○ ○ ○ ○

"It is impossible to live without failing at something, unless you live so cautiously that you might as well not have lived at all – in which case, you fail by default."

J. K. ROWLING

○ ○ ○ ○ ○ ○ ○ ○ ○ ○
○ ○ ○ ○ ○ ○ ○ ○ ○ ○
○ ○ ○ ○ ○ ○ ○ ○ ○ ○
○ ○ ○ ○ ○ ○ ○ ○ ○ ○
○ ○ ○ ○ ○ ○ ○ ○ ○ ○
○ ○ ○ ○ ○ ○ ○ ○ ○ ○
○ ○ ○ ○ ○ ○ ○ ○ ○ ○
○ ○ ○ ○ ○ ○ ○ ○ ○ ○
○ ○ ○ ○ ○ ○ ○ ○ ○ ○

"Debt erases freedom more surely than anything else."

MERRYN SOMERSET WEBB

90 Day Habit Release

○ ○ ○ ○ ○ ○ ○ ○ ○ ○
○ ○ ○ ○ ○ ○ ○ ○ ○ ○
○ ○ ○ ○ ○ ○ ○ ○ ○ ○
○ ○ ○ ○ ○ ○ ○ ○ ○ ○
○ ○ ○ ○ ○ ○ ○ ○ ○ ○
○ ○ ○ ○ ○ ○ ○ ○ ○ ○
○ ○ ○ ○ ○ ○ ○ ○ ○ ○
○ ○ ○ ○ ○ ○ ○ ○ ○ ○
○ ○ ○ ○ ○ ○ ○ ○ ○ ○

"The truth is, you don't break a bad habit; you replace it with a good one."

DENIS WAITLEY

MONDAY	
TIME:	**ACTION:**
am	
9am	
10am	
11am	
12pm	
1pm	
2pm	

Evening:

Dinner:

todays win

TUESDAY	
TIME:	**ACTION:**
am	
9am	
10am	
11am	
12pm	
1pm	
2pm	

Evening:

Dinner:

todays win

WEDNESDAY

TIME:	ACTION:
am	
9am	
10am	
11am	
12pm	
1pm	
2pm	

Evening:

Dinner:

todays win

THURSDAY

TIME:	ACTION:
am	
9am	
10am	
11am	
12pm	
1pm	
2pm	

Evening:

Dinner:

todays win

FRIDAY

TIME:	ACTION:
am	
9am	
10am	
11am	
12pm	
1pm	
2pm	

WEEKEND:

TIME:	ACTION:

DITCH, DELEGATE, DO NEXT WEEK:

Evening:

Dinner:

todays win

Next weeks #1 Goal

weekend wins

MONDAY		TUESDAY	
TIME:	**ACTION:**	**TIME:**	**ACTION:**
am		am	
9am		9am	
10am		10am	
11am		11am	
12pm		12pm	
1pm		1pm	
2pm		2pm	

Evening:

Dinner:

Evening:

Dinner:

todays win

todays win

WEDNESDAY		THURSDAY	
TIME:	**ACTION:**	**TIME:**	**ACTION:**
am		am	
9am		9am	
10am		10am	
11am		11am	
12pm		12pm	
1pm		1pm	
2pm		2pm	

Evening:

Evening:

Dinner:

Dinner:

todays *win*

todays *win*

FRIDAY		WEEKEND:	
TIME:	**ACTION:**	**TIME:**	**ACTION:**
am			
9am			
10am			
11am			

DITCH, DELEGATE, DO NEXT WEEK:

12pm			
1pm			
2pm			

Evening:

Dinner:

Next weeks #1 Goal

todays win

weekend wins

MONDAY		TUESDAY	
TIME:	**ACTION:**	**TIME:**	**ACTION:**
am		am	
9am		9am	
10am		10am	
11am		11am	
12pm		12pm	
1pm		1pm	
2pm		2pm	

Evening:

Evening:

Dinner:

Dinner:

todays win

todays win

WEDNESDAY

TIME:	ACTION:
am	
9am	
10am	
11am	
12pm	
1pm	
2pm	

Evening:

Dinner:

todays win

THURSDAY

TIME:	ACTION:
am	
9am	
10am	
11am	
12pm	
1pm	
2pm	

Evening:

Dinner:

todays win

FRIDAY		WEEKEND:	
TIME:	**ACTION:**	**TIME:**	**ACTION:**
am			
9am			
10am			
11am			
		DITCH, DELEGATE, DO NEXT WEEK:	
12pm			
1pm			
2pm			

Evening:

Dinner:

todays win

Next weeks #1 Goal

weekend wins

MONDAY

TIME:	ACTION:
am	
9am	
10am	
11am	
12pm	
1pm	
2pm	

Evening:

Dinner:

todays win

TUESDAY

TIME:	ACTION:
am	
9am	
10am	
11am	
12pm	
1pm	
2pm	

Evening:

Dinner:

todays win

WEDNESDAY		THURSDAY	
TIME:	ACTION:	TIME:	ACTION:
am		am	
9am		9am	
10am		10am	
11am		11am	
12pm		12pm	
1pm		1pm	
2pm		2pm	

Evening:

Dinner:

todays win

Evening:

Dinner:

todays win

FRIDAY

TIME:	ACTION:
am	
9am	
10am	
11am	
12pm	
1pm	
2pm	

Evening:

Dinner:

todays win

WEEKEND:

TIME:	ACTION:

DITCH, DELEGATE, DO NEXT WEEK:

Next weeks #1 Goal

weekend wins

MONDAY		TUESDAY	
TIME:	**ACTION:**	**TIME:**	**ACTION:**
am		am	
9am		9am	
10am		10am	
11am		11am	
12pm		12pm	
1pm		1pm	
2pm		2pm	

Evening:

Evening:

Dinner:

Dinner:

todays win

todays win

WEDNESDAY		THURSDAY	
TIME:	ACTION:	TIME:	ACTION:
am		am	
9am		9am	
10am		10am	
11am		11am	
12pm		12pm	
1pm		1pm	
2pm		2pm	

Evening:

Evening:

Dinner:

Dinner:

todays win

todays win

FRIDAY		WEEKEND:	
TIME:	**ACTION:**	**TIME:**	**ACTION:**
am			
9am			
10am			
11am			
			DITCH, DELEGATE, DO NEXT WEEK:
12pm			
1pm			
2pm			

Evening:

Dinner:

Next weeks
#1
goal

todays
win

weekend
wins

MONDAY		TUESDAY	
TIME:	ACTION:	TIME:	ACTION:
am		am	
9am		9am	
10am		10am	
11am		11am	
12pm		12pm	
1pm		1pm	
2pm		2pm	

Evening:

Evening:

Dinner:

Dinner:

todays win

todays win

WEDNESDAY		THURSDAY	
TIME:	**ACTION:**	**TIME:**	**ACTION:**
am		am	
9am		9am	
10am		10am	
11am		11am	
12pm		12pm	
1pm		1pm	
2pm		2pm	

Evening:

Evening:

Dinner:

Dinner:

todays win

todays win

FRIDAY

TIME:	ACTION:
am	
9am	
10am	
11am	
12pm	
1pm	
2pm	

Evening:

Dinner:

todays win

WEEKEND:

TIME:	ACTION:

DITCH, DELEGATE, DO NEXT WEEK:

Next weeks #1 Goal

weekend wins

MONDAY		TUESDAY	
TIME:	ACTION:	TIME:	ACTION:
am		am	
9am		9am	
10am		10am	
11am		11am	
12pm		12pm	
1pm		1pm	
2pm		2pm	

Evening:

Dinner:

todays win

Evening:

Dinner:

todays win

WEDNESDAY	
TIME:	ACTION:
am	
9am	
10am	
11am	
12pm	
1pm	
2pm	

Evening:

Dinner:

todays win

THURSDAY	
TIME:	ACTION:
am	
9am	
10am	
11am	
12pm	
1pm	
2pm	

Evening:

Dinner:

todays win

FRIDAY		WEEKEND:	
TIME:	**ACTION:**	**TIME:**	**ACTION:**
am			
9am			
10am			
11am			

DITCH, DELEGATE, DO NEXT WEEK:

12pm			
1pm			
2pm			

Evening:

Next weeks #1 Goal

Dinner:

todays win

weekend wins

MONDAY			TUESDAY	
TIME:	**ACTION:**		**TIME:**	**ACTION:**
am			am	
9am			9am	
10am			10am	
11am			11am	
12pm			12pm	
1pm			1pm	
2pm			2pm	

Evening:

Dinner:

Evening:

Dinner:

todays win

todays win

WEDNESDAY

TIME:	ACTION:
am	
9am	
10am	
11am	
12pm	
1pm	
2pm	

Evening:

Dinner:

todays win

THURSDAY

TIME:	ACTION:
am	
9am	
10am	
11am	
12pm	
1pm	
2pm	

Evening:

Dinner:

todays win

FRIDAY		WEEKEND:	
TIME:	**ACTION:**	**TIME:**	**ACTION:**
am			
9am			
10am			
11am			
		DITCH, DELEGATE, DO NEXT WEEK:	
12pm			
1pm			
2pm			

Evening:

Dinner:

todays win

Next weeks #1 Goal

weekend wins

MONDAY		TUESDAY	
TIME:	**ACTION:**	**TIME:**	**ACTION:**
am		am	
9am		9am	
10am		10am	
11am		11am	
12pm		12pm	
1pm		1pm	
2pm		2pm	

Evening:

Dinner:

todays win

Evening:

Dinner:

todays win

WEDNESDAY		THURSDAY	
TIME:	**ACTION:**	**TIME:**	**ACTION:**
am		am	
9am		9am	
10am		10am	
11am		11am	
12pm		12pm	
1pm		1pm	
2pm		2pm	

Evening:

Evening:

Dinner:

Dinner:

todays win

todays win

FRIDAY

TIME:	ACTION:
am	
9am	
10am	
11am	
12pm	
1pm	
2pm	

Evening:

Dinner:

todays win

WEEKEND:

TIME:	ACTION:

DITCH, DELEGATE, DO NEXT WEEK:

Next weeks #1 Goal

weekend wins

MONDAY		TUESDAY	
TIME:	**ACTION:**	**TIME:**	**ACTION:**
am		am	
9am		9am	
10am		10am	
11am		11am	
12pm		12pm	
1pm		1pm	
2pm		2pm	

Evening:

Evening:

Dinner:

Dinner:

todays win

todays win

WEDNESDAY		THURSDAY	
TIME:	**ACTION:**	**TIME:**	**ACTION:**
am		am	
9am		9am	
10am		10am	
11am		11am	
12pm		12pm	
1pm		1pm	
2pm		2pm	

Evening:

Evening:

Dinner:

Dinner:

todays win

todays win

FRIDAY

TIME:	ACTION:
am	
9am	
10am	
11am	
12pm	
1pm	
2pm	

Evening:

Dinner:

todays win

WEEKEND:

TIME:	ACTION:

DITCH, DELEGATE, DO NEXT WEEK:

Next weeks #1 Goal

weekend wins

MONDAY

TIME:	ACTION:
am	
9am	
10am	
11am	
12pm	
1pm	
2pm	

Evening:

Dinner:

todays win

TUESDAY

TIME:	ACTION:
am	
9am	
10am	
11am	
12pm	
1pm	
2pm	

Evening:

Dinner:

todays win

WEDNESDAY		THURSDAY	
TIME:	**ACTION:**	**TIME:**	**ACTION:**
am		**am**	
9am		**9am**	
10am		**10am**	
11am		**11am**	
12pm		**12pm**	
1pm		**1pm**	
2pm		**2pm**	

Evening:

Dinner:

todays win

Evening:

Dinner:

todays win

FRIDAY

TIME:	ACTION:
am	
9am	
10am	
11am	
12pm	
1pm	
2pm	

Evening:

Dinner:

todays win

WEEKEND:

TIME:	ACTION:

DITCH, DELEGATE, DO NEXT WEEK:

Next weeks
#1
Goal

weekend wins

MONDAY		TUESDAY	
TIME:	**ACTION:**	**TIME:**	**ACTION:**
am		am	
9am		9am	
10am		10am	
11am		11am	
12pm		12pm	
1pm		1pm	
2pm		2pm	

Evening:

Evening:

Dinner:

Dinner:

todays win

todays win

WEDNESDAY		THURSDAY	
TIME:	**ACTION:**	**TIME:**	**ACTION:**
am		am	
9am		9am	
10am		10am	
11am		11am	
12pm		12pm	
1pm		1pm	
2pm		2pm	

Evening:

Dinner:

todays win

Evening:

Dinner:

todays win

FRIDAY			WEEKEND:	
TIME:	**ACTION:**		**TIME:**	**ACTION:**
am				
9am				
10am				
11am				

DITCH, DELEGATE, DO NEXT WEEK:

FRIDAY	
12pm	
1pm	
2pm	

Evening:

Dinner:

Next weeks **#1** *Goal*

todays *win*

weekend *wins*

MONDAY		TUESDAY	
TIME:	**ACTION:**	**TIME:**	**ACTION:**
am		am	
9am		9am	
10am		10am	
11am		11am	
12pm		12pm	
1pm		1pm	
2pm		2pm	

Evening:

Dinner:

todays win

Evening:

Dinner:

todays win

WEDNESDAY		THURSDAY	
TIME:	**ACTION:**	**TIME:**	**ACTION:**
am		am	
9am		9am	
10am		10am	
11am		11am	
12pm		12pm	
1pm		1pm	
2pm		2pm	

Evening:

Evening:

Dinner:

Dinner:

todays win

todays win

FRIDAY		WEEKEND:	
TIME:	**ACTION:**	**TIME:**	**ACTION:**
am			
9am			
10am			
11am			

DITCH, DELEGATE, DO NEXT WEEK:

12pm			
1pm			
2pm			

Evening:

Next weeks
#1
Goal

Dinner:

todays win

weekend wins

MONDAY		TUESDAY	
TIME:	**ACTION:**	**TIME:**	**ACTION:**
am		am	
9am		9am	
10am		10am	
11am		11am	
12pm		12pm	
1pm		1pm	
2pm		2pm	

Evening:

Dinner:

Evening:

Dinner:

todays win

todays win

WEDNESDAY		THURSDAY	
TIME:	**ACTION:**	**TIME:**	**ACTION:**
am		am	
9am		9am	
10am		10am	
11am		11am	
12pm		12pm	
1pm		1pm	
2pm		2pm	

Evening:

Dinner:

Evening:

Dinner:

todays win

todays win

FRIDAY		WEEKEND:	
TIME:	**ACTION:**	**TIME:**	**ACTION:**
am			
9am			
10am			
11am			

DITCH, DELEGATE, DO NEXT WEEK:

FRIDAY	
12pm	
1pm	
2pm	

Evening:

Next weeks #1 goal

Dinner:

todays win

weekend wins

MONDAY		TUESDAY	
TIME:	**ACTION:**	**TIME:**	**ACTION:**
am		am	
9am		9am	
10am		10am	
11am		11am	
12pm		12pm	
1pm		1pm	
2pm		2pm	

Evening:

Evening:

Dinner:

Dinner:

todays win

todays win

WEDNESDAY		THURSDAY	
TIME:	**ACTION:**	**TIME:**	**ACTION:**
am		am	
9am		9am	
10am		10am	
11am		11am	
12pm		12pm	
1pm		1pm	
2pm		2pm	

Evening:

Evening:

Dinner:

Dinner:

todays win

todays win

FRIDAY		WEEKEND:	
TIME:	**ACTION:**	**TIME:**	**ACTION:**
am			
9am			
10am			
11am			

DITCH, DELEGATE, DO NEXT WEEK:

12pm			
1pm			
2pm			

Evening:

Next weeks #1 Goal

Dinner:

todays win

weekend wins

Goal Setting, Reflection & Review

What was my #1 Goal for this 12 months?

_____

_____

Have I achieved the goals I set for months 7, 8 & 9?

_____

_____

_____

My key wins have been:

_____

_____

_____

My key challenges have been:

_____

_____

_____

My key learnings are:

_____

_____

_____

Do I need to adjust my 12 month #1 Goal?

_____

_____

_____

My #1 Goal for the next 90 days is:

_____

_____

_____

My #1 Goal for month 10:

_____

My #1 Goal for month 11:

_____

My #1 Goal for month 12:

_____

90 Day Habit Tracker

○ ○ ○ ○ ○ ○ ○ ○ ○ ○
○ ○ ○ ○ ○ ○ ○ ○ ○ ○
○ ○ ○ ○ ○ ○ ○ ○ ○ ○
○ ○ ○ ○ ○ ○ ○ ○ ○ ○
○ ○ ○ ○ ○ ○ ○ ○ ○ ○
○ ○ ○ ○ ○ ○ ○ ○ ○ ○
○ ○ ○ ○ ○ ○ ○ ○ ○ ○
○ ○ ○ ○ ○ ○ ○ ○ ○ ○
○ ○ ○ ○ ○ ○ ○ ○ ○ ○

"A strong woman looks a challenge dead in the eye & gives it a wink."

GINA CAREY

○ ○ ○ ○ ○ ○ ○ ○ ○ ○
○ ○ ○ ○ ○ ○ ○ ○ ○ ○
○ ○ ○ ○ ○ ○ ○ ○ ○ ○
○ ○ ○ ○ ○ ○ ○ ○ ○ ○
○ ○ ○ ○ ○ ○ ○ ○ ○ ○
○ ○ ○ ○ ○ ○ ○ ○ ○ ○
○ ○ ○ ○ ○ ○ ○ ○ ○ ○
○ ○ ○ ○ ○ ○ ○ ○ ○ ○
○ ○ ○ ○ ○ ○ ○ ○ ○ ○

"It isn't until you come to a spiritual understanding of who you are, deep down, that you can begin to take control."

OPRAH WINFREY

○ ○ ○ ○ ○ ○ ○ ○ ○ ○
○ ○ ○ ○ ○ ○ ○ ○ ○ ○
○ ○ ○ ○ ○ ○ ○ ○ ○ ○
○ ○ ○ ○ ○ ○ ○ ○ ○ ○
○ ○ ○ ○ ○ ○ ○ ○ ○ ○
○ ○ ○ ○ ○ ○ ○ ○ ○ ○
○ ○ ○ ○ ○ ○ ○ ○ ○ ○
○ ○ ○ ○ ○ ○ ○ ○ ○ ○
○ ○ ○ ○ ○ ○ ○ ○ ○ ○

"Every job is a self-portrait of the person who does it. Autograph your work with excellence."

ANONYMOUS

○ ○ ○ ○ ○ ○ ○ ○ ○ ○
○ ○ ○ ○ ○ ○ ○ ○ ○ ○
○ ○ ○ ○ ○ ○ ○ ○ ○ ○
○ ○ ○ ○ ○ ○ ○ ○ ○ ○
○ ○ ○ ○ ○ ○ ○ ○ ○ ○
○ ○ ○ ○ ○ ○ ○ ○ ○ ○
○ ○ ○ ○ ○ ○ ○ ○ ○ ○
○ ○ ○ ○ ○ ○ ○ ○ ○ ○
○ ○ ○ ○ ○ ○ ○ ○ ○ ○

"It's never too late to be what you might have been."

GEORGE ELIOT

○ ○ ○ ○ ○ ○ ○ ○ ○ ○
○ ○ ○ ○ ○ ○ ○ ○ ○ ○
○ ○ ○ ○ ○ ○ ○ ○ ○ ○
○ ○ ○ ○ ○ ○ ○ ○ ○ ○
○ ○ ○ ○ ○ ○ ○ ○ ○ ○
○ ○ ○ ○ ○ ○ ○ ○ ○ ○
○ ○ ○ ○ ○ ○ ○ ○ ○ ○
○ ○ ○ ○ ○ ○ ○ ○ ○ ○
○ ○ ○ ○ ○ ○ ○ ○ ○ ○

"Those who do not find time for exercise will have to find time for illness."

EARL OF DERBY

90 Day Habit Release

○ ○ ○ ○ ○ ○ ○ ○ ○ ○
○ ○ ○ ○ ○ ○ ○ ○ ○ ○
○ ○ ○ ○ ○ ○ ○ ○ ○ ○
○ ○ ○ ○ ○ ○ ○ ○ ○ ○
○ ○ ○ ○ ○ ○ ○ ○ ○ ○
○ ○ ○ ○ ○ ○ ○ ○ ○ ○
○ ○ ○ ○ ○ ○ ○ ○ ○ ○
○ ○ ○ ○ ○ ○ ○ ○ ○ ○
○ ○ ○ ○ ○ ○ ○ ○ ○ ○

"A bad habit never disappears miraculously, it's an undo-it-yourself project."

ABIGAIL VAN BUREN

MONDAY		TUESDAY	
TIME:	**ACTION:**	**TIME:**	**ACTION:**
am		am	
9am		9am	
10am		10am	
11am		11am	
12pm		12pm	
1pm		1pm	
2pm		2pm	

Evening:

Evening:

Dinner:

Dinner:

todays win

todays win

WEDNESDAY	
TIME:	**ACTION:**
am	
9am	
10am	
11am	
12pm	
1pm	
2pm	

Evening:

Dinner:

todays win

THURSDAY	
TIME:	**ACTION:**
am	
9am	
10am	
11am	
12pm	
1pm	
2pm	

Evening:

Dinner:

todays win

FRIDAY

TIME:	ACTION:
am	
9am	
10am	
11am	
12pm	
1pm	
2pm	

Evening:

Dinner:

todays win

WEEKEND:

TIME:	ACTION:

DITCH, DELEGATE, DO NEXT WEEK:

Next weeks #1 Goal

weekend wins

MONDAY		TUESDAY	
TIME:	**ACTION:**	**TIME:**	**ACTION:**
am		am	
9am		9am	
10am		10am	
11am		11am	
12pm		12pm	
1pm		1pm	
2pm		2pm	

Evening:

Dinner:

Evening:

Dinner:

todays win

todays win

WEDNESDAY		THURSDAY	
TIME:	**ACTION:**	**TIME:**	**ACTION:**
am		am	
9am		9am	
10am		10am	
11am		11am	
12pm		12pm	
1pm		1pm	
2pm		2pm	

Evening:

Evening:

Dinner:

Dinner:

todays win

todays win

FRIDAY		WEEKEND:	
TIME:	ACTION:	TIME:	ACTION:
am			
9am			
10am			
11am			

DITCH, DELEGATE, DO NEXT WEEK:

12pm			
1pm			
2pm			

Evening:

Next weeks #1 Goal

Dinner:

todays win

weekend wins

MONDAY		TUESDAY	
TIME:	**ACTION:**	**TIME:**	**ACTION:**
am		am	
9am		9am	
10am		10am	
11am		11am	
12pm		12pm	
1pm		1pm	
2pm		2pm	

Evening:

Dinner:

todays win

Evening:

Dinner:

todays win

WEDNESDAY		THURSDAY	
TIME:	**ACTION:**	**TIME:**	**ACTION:**
am		**am**	
9am		**9am**	
10am		**10am**	
11am		**11am**	
12pm		**12pm**	
1pm		**1pm**	
2pm		**2pm**	

Evening:

Dinner:

Evening:

Dinner:

todays win

todays win

FRIDAY

TIME:	ACTION:
am	
9am	
10am	
11am	
12pm	
1pm	
2pm	

Evening:

Dinner:

todays win

WEEKEND:

TIME:	ACTION:

DITCH, DELEGATE, DO NEXT WEEK:

Next weeks #1 Goal

weekend wins

MONDAY		TUESDAY	
TIME:	**ACTION:**	**TIME:**	**ACTION:**
am		**am**	
9am		**9am**	
10am		**10am**	
11am		**11am**	
12pm		**12pm**	
1pm		**1pm**	
2pm		**2pm**	

Evening:

Dinner:

todays win

Evening:

Dinner:

todays win

WEDNESDAY		THURSDAY	
TIME:	**ACTION:**	**TIME:**	**ACTION:**
am		am	
9am		9am	
10am		10am	
11am		11am	
12pm		12pm	
1pm		1pm	
2pm		2pm	

Evening:

Dinner:

todays win

Evening:

Dinner:

todays win

FRIDAY

TIME:	ACTION:
am	
9am	
10am	
11am	
12pm	
1pm	
2pm	

Evening:

Dinner:

todays win

WEEKEND:

TIME:	ACTION:

DITCH, DELEGATE, DO NEXT WEEK:

Next weeks #1 Goal

weekend wins

MONDAY		TUESDAY	
TIME:	**ACTION:**	**TIME:**	**ACTION:**
am		am	
9am		9am	
10am		10am	
11am		11am	
12pm		12pm	
1pm		1pm	
2pm		2pm	

Evening:

Dinner:

todays win

Evening:

Dinner:

todays win

WEDNESDAY		THURSDAY	
TIME:	**ACTION:**	**TIME:**	**ACTION:**
am		am	
9am		9am	
10am		10am	
11am		11am	
12pm		12pm	
1pm		1pm	
2pm		2pm	

Evening:

Dinner:

Evening:

Dinner:

todays win

todays win

FRIDAY		WEEKEND:	
TIME:	**ACTION:**	**TIME:**	**ACTION:**
am			
9am			
10am			
11am			

DITCH, DELEGATE, DO NEXT WEEK:

12pm			
1pm			
2pm			

Evening:

Next weeks #1 Goal

Dinner:

todays win

weekend wins

MONDAY		TUESDAY	
TIME:	**ACTION:**	**TIME:**	**ACTION:**
am		am	
9am		9am	
10am		10am	
11am		11am	
12pm		12pm	
1pm		1pm	
2pm		2pm	

Evening:

Dinner:

Evening:

Dinner:

todays win

todays win

WEDNESDAY		THURSDAY	
TIME:	**ACTION:**	**TIME:**	**ACTION:**
am		am	
9am		9am	
10am		10am	
11am		11am	
12pm		12pm	
1pm		1pm	
2pm		2pm	

Evening:

Evening:

Dinner:

Dinner:

todays win

todays win

FRIDAY

TIME:	ACTION:
am	
9am	
10am	
11am	
12pm	
1pm	
2pm	

Evening:

Dinner:

todays win

WEEKEND:

TIME:	ACTION:

DITCH, DELEGATE, DO NEXT WEEK:

Next weeks #1 Goal

weekend wins

MONDAY			TUESDAY	
TIME:	ACTION:		TIME:	ACTION:
am			am	
9am			9am	
10am			10am	
11am			11am	
12pm			12pm	
1pm			1pm	
2pm			2pm	

Evening:

Evening:

Dinner:

Dinner:

todays win

todays win

WEDNESDAY		THURSDAY	
TIME:	**ACTION:**	**TIME:**	**ACTION:**
am		am	
9am		9am	
10am		10am	
11am		11am	
12pm		12pm	
1pm		1pm	
2pm		2pm	

Evening:

Dinner:

Evening:

Dinner:

todays win *todays win*

FRIDAY

TIME:	ACTION:
am	
9am	
10am	
11am	
12pm	
1pm	
2pm	

Evening:

Dinner:

todays win

WEEKEND:

TIME:	ACTION:

DITCH, DELEGATE, DO NEXT WEEK:

Next weeks #1 Goal

weekend wins

MONDAY

TIME:	ACTION:
am	
9am	
10am	
11am	
12pm	
1pm	
2pm	

Evening:

Dinner:

todays win

TUESDAY

TIME:	ACTION:
am	
9am	
10am	
11am	
12pm	
1pm	
2pm	

Evening:

Dinner:

todays win

WEDNESDAY		THURSDAY	
TIME:	**ACTION:**	**TIME:**	**ACTION:**
am		am	
9am		9am	
10am		10am	
11am		11am	
12pm		12pm	
1pm		1pm	
2pm		2pm	

Evening:

Evening:

Dinner:

Dinner:

todays win

todays win

FRIDAY		WEEKEND:	
TIME:	**ACTION:**	**TIME:**	**ACTION:**
am			
9am			
10am			
11am			

DITCH, DELEGATE, DO NEXT WEEK:

12pm			
1pm			
2pm			

Evening:

Next weeks #1 Goal

Dinner:

todays win

weekend wins

MONDAY		TUESDAY	
TIME:	**ACTION:**	**TIME:**	**ACTION:**
am		am	
9am		9am	
10am		10am	
11am		11am	
12pm		12pm	
1pm		1pm	
2pm		2pm	

Evening:

Dinner:

Evening:

Dinner:

todays win

todays win

WEDNESDAY		THURSDAY	
TIME:	**ACTION:**	**TIME:**	**ACTION:**
am		am	
9am		9am	
10am		10am	
11am		11am	
12pm		12pm	
1pm		1pm	
2pm		2pm	

Evening:

Evening:

Dinner:

Dinner:

todays win

todays win

FRIDAY		WEEKEND:	
TIME:	**ACTION:**	**TIME:**	**ACTION:**
am			
9am			
10am			
11am			

	DITCH, DELEGATE, DO NEXT WEEK:
12pm	
1pm	
2pm	

Evening:

Dinner:

todays win

Next weeks #1 Goal

weekend wins

MONDAY		TUESDAY	
TIME:	**ACTION:**	**TIME:**	**ACTION:**
am		am	
9am		9am	
10am		10am	
11am		11am	
12pm		12pm	
1pm		1pm	
2pm		2pm	

Evening:

Evening:

Dinner:

Dinner:

todays win

todays win

WEDNESDAY		THURSDAY	
TIME:	ACTION:	TIME:	ACTION:
am		am	
9am		9am	
10am		10am	
11am		11am	
12pm		12pm	
1pm		1pm	
2pm		2pm	

Evening:

Dinner:

Evening:

Dinner:

todays win

todays win

FRIDAY		WEEKEND:	
TIME:	**ACTION:**	**TIME:**	**ACTION:**
am			
9am			
10am			
11am			
		DITCH, DELEGATE, DO NEXT WEEK:	
12pm			
1pm			
2pm			

Evening:

Dinner:

todays win

Next weeks #1 Goal

weekend wins

MONDAY		TUESDAY	
TIME:	**ACTION:**	**TIME:**	**ACTION:**
am		am	
9am		9am	
10am		10am	
11am		11am	
12pm		12pm	
1pm		1pm	
2pm		2pm	

Evening:

Dinner:

Evening:

Dinner:

todays win

todays win

WEDNESDAY		THURSDAY	
TIME:	**ACTION:**	**TIME:**	**ACTION:**
am		am	
9am		9am	
10am		10am	
11am		11am	
12pm		12pm	
1pm		1pm	
2pm		2pm	

Evening:

Dinner:

Evening:

Dinner:

todays win

todays win

FRIDAY

TIME:	ACTION:
am	
9am	
10am	
11am	
12pm	
1pm	
2pm	

Evening:

Dinner:

todays win

WEEKEND:

TIME:	ACTION:

DITCH, DELEGATE, DO NEXT WEEK:

Next weeks #1 Goal

weekend wins

MONDAY	
TIME:	**ACTION:**
am	
9am	
10am	
11am	
12pm	
1pm	
2pm	

Evening:

Dinner:

todays win

TUESDAY	
TIME:	**ACTION:**
am	
9am	
10am	
11am	
12pm	
1pm	
2pm	

Evening:

Dinner:

todays win

WEDNESDAY	
TIME:	ACTION:
am	
9am	
10am	
11am	
12pm	
1pm	
2pm	

Evening:

Dinner:

todays win

THURSDAY	
TIME:	ACTION:
am	
9am	
10am	
11am	
12pm	
1pm	
2pm	

Evening:

Dinner:

todays win

FRIDAY		WEEKEND:	
TIME:	**ACTION:**	**TIME:**	**ACTION:**
am			
9am			
10am			
11am			

DITCH, DELEGATE, DO NEXT WEEK:

FRIDAY			
12pm			
1pm			
2pm			

Evening:

Next weeks #1 goal

Dinner:

todays win

weekend wins

MONDAY

TIME:	ACTION:
am	
9am	
10am	
11am	
12pm	
1pm	
2pm	

Evening:

Dinner:

todays win

TUESDAY

TIME:	ACTION:
am	
9am	
10am	
11am	
12pm	
1pm	
2pm	

Evening:

Dinner:

todays win

WEDNESDAY		THURSDAY	
TIME:	**ACTION:**	**TIME:**	**ACTION:**
am		am	
9am		9am	
10am		10am	
11am		11am	
12pm		12pm	
1pm		1pm	
2pm		2pm	

Evening:

Dinner:

Evening:

Dinner:

todays win

todays win

FRIDAY		WEEKEND:	
TIME:	**ACTION:**	**TIME:**	**ACTION:**
am			
9am			
10am			
11am			
		DITCH, DELEGATE, DO NEXT WEEK:	
12pm			
1pm			
2pm			

Evening:

Next weeks #1 Goal

Dinner:

todays win

weekend wins

MONDAY		TUESDAY	
TIME:	**ACTION:**	**TIME:**	**ACTION:**
am		am	
9am		9am	
10am		10am	
11am		11am	
12pm		12pm	
1pm		1pm	
2pm		2pm	

Evening:

Dinner:

Evening:

Dinner:

todays win

todays win

WEDNESDAY		THURSDAY	
TIME:	**ACTION:**	**TIME:**	**ACTION:**
am		am	
9am		9am	
10am		10am	
11am		11am	
12pm		12pm	
1pm		1pm	
2pm		2pm	

Evening:

Dinner:

Evening:

Dinner:

todays win

todays win

FRIDAY		WEEKEND:	
TIME:	**ACTION:**	**TIME:**	**ACTION:**
am			
9am			
10am			
11am			
		DITCH, DELEGATE, DO NEXT WEEK:	
12pm			
1pm			
2pm			

Evening:

Dinner:

Next weeks #1 Goal

todays win

weekend wins

MONDAY		TUESDAY	
TIME:	**ACTION:**	**TIME:**	**ACTION:**
am		am	
9am		9am	
10am		10am	
11am		11am	
12pm		12pm	
1pm		1pm	
2pm		2pm	

Evening:

Dinner:

Evening:

Dinner:

todays win

todays win

WEDNESDAY

TIME:	ACTION:
am	
9am	
10am	
11am	
12pm	
1pm	
2pm	

Evening:

Dinner:

todays win

THURSDAY

TIME:	ACTION:
am	
9am	
10am	
11am	
12pm	
1pm	
2pm	

Evening:

Dinner:

todays win

FRIDAY

TIME:	ACTION:
am	
9am	
10am	
11am	
12pm	
1pm	
2pm	

Evening:

Dinner:

todays win

WEEKEND:

TIME:	ACTION:

DITCH, DELEGATE, DO NEXT WEEK:

Next weeks #1 Goal

weekend wins

Goal Setting, Reflection & Review

What was my #1 Goal for this 12 months?

_____

_____

_____

Have I achieved the goals I set for months 10, 11 & 12?

_____

_____

_____

My key wins have been:

_____

_____

_____

My key challenges have been:

_____

_____

_____

My key learnings are:

_____

_____

_____

What is my #1 Goal for the next 12 months?

_____

_____

_____

My #1 Goal for the next 90 days is:

_____

_____

_____

My #1 Goal for month 1:

_____

My #1 Goal for month 2:

_____

My #1 Goal for month 3:

_____

You did it!

Congratulations on developing this habit!

Life moves pretty fast, sometimes we're so consumed that we forget to savour the wins along the way. Remember to take time to reflect on how far you've come, celebrate your successes and enjoy the journey.

You dared to dream, you've worked hard, you are one of life's inspiring characters!

Scan the QR Code below to grab your next one and think ahead to what the future holds for you.

Pippa x

"We are what we repeatedly do.
Excellence, then, is not an act, but a habit."
Aristotle